VITAL LIVING

tidy

for a calmer you

RED WHEEL

This edition first published in 2023 by Red Wheel,
an imprint of Red Wheel/Weiser, llc
With offices at:
65 Parker Street, Suite 7, Newburyport, MA 01950
www.redwheelweiser.com

ISBN: 978-1-59003-554-2

Library of Congress Cataloging-in-Publication Data available
upon request.

Author: Becky Dickinson
Cover design: Milestone Creative
Contents design: Jo Ross, Double Fish Design Ltd
Illustrations: under licence from Shutterstock.com

Printed in China

10 9 8 7 6 5 4 3 2 1

contents

Have nothing in your
house that you do not
know to be useful, or
believe to be beautiful.

WILLIAM MORRIS

introduction

Do you long for a clean and organized house? Do you try to spring clean every season of the year, yet still find yourself surrounded by clutter? An untidy home can have a profound impact on your sense of calm, making you feel anxious and overwhelmed. Clutter isn't just physical – it is emotional and spiritual too. This book will show you how to tidy your life, conquering a task that might initially appear like a mountain. You'll discover how to dispose of things you don't need and how to reorganize the things that you do. You'll also learn how to make this a mindset for life, so that you can keep your home and your life clutter-free with minimum effort. With practical tips for tidying different areas of your home, and insights into the emotional side of hoarding, this book will give you back control of both your living space and your life.

the age-old battle to be tidy

What makes us feel the need to be tidy? As humans, we're naturally inclined to try to make sense of the chaos around us. Science, philosophy and religion have been trying to give existence a framework for thousands of years. For some people, creating order means making lists; for others it's wearing perfectly ironed clothes. But how deep does this desire for order go? Has it always been in our genes? Experts in human evolution believe that it has.

Scientists believe that humans organized their living spaces a long, long time before Marie Kondo came along. In fact, they flag it as one of the hallmarks of human behavior. In 2009, archaeologists in Israel got to work on an 800,000-year-old site belonging to our ancient human ancestors. What they found suggested that our desire to organize has even deeper evolutionary roots than previously thought.

Excavations revealed that activities on the site – for example tool-making and food consumption – were concentrated in different areas. The designation of areas for different activities shows a clear division of living space. For example, you wouldn't find yourself sleeping next to fishbones or making stone tools in the basalt tool-making area. It turns out that our ancestors were much more sophisticated than we previously gave them credit for. Perhaps Kondomari isn't just a 21st-century phenomenon!

Aside from the practical side of organizing our living spaces, the emotional side also has deep roots. Over millions of years, our propensity to make things and find shelter has made us homebodies. Feelings for home bring comfort and security. Our human predecessors stopped moving around so much and started to make homes that became a focus for sharing food and bringing up children – the latter especially requiring security and stability in what could in those days be a dangerous world. Through the years and as we evolved, a sense of home became vitally important to us – we need a home just as much as we need food. It's a psychological need, which is why creating a space around us that is tidy and organized is so important to our well-being.

If we're an inherently tidy species, then why do we collect clutter in the first place?

Pressure on us as consumers: you must buy this, that or the other, or else your life won't be complete. Or so retailers and the media tell us.

●

For the future: this could include stockpiling items for fear you won't be able to get them in the future (or in anticipation of a zombie apocalypse!) or because you have plans for a different future life in mind.

•

Guilt and obligation: for example, all those gifts and hand-me-downs you've received from a loved one which you've felt too guilty to do anything with but keep.

•

An emotional attachment to the past: things you can't bear to part with because they hold a special memory or emotional significance.

•

Building collections: sometimes what starts off as an innocent collection gets out of hand. We've all seen magazine articles about the person who started off collecting teddy bears and now can't move in their home for their furry friends!

Humans are emotional beings. We therefore also tend to attach emotion to our possessions. They become part of us and are therefore incredibly hard to dispose of. We joke that when someone loses their cell phone, they feel completely at sea – 'It felt like having my limb cut off'. But it's a very real feeling of loss as we rely so much on our phones as a way of connecting to the world. So many of our belongings become an extension of ourselves that we think we would be lost without them. In reality, surrounding yourself with too much 'stuff' has the opposite effect – it doesn't create calm, it creates turbulence.

Coming home to a tidy,
pulled-together space
will help everything
in your life feel the
same way.

BOBBY BERK

the emotional toll of clutter

It isn't always easy to control what is happening in the world around us, whether that be work, friendships or family life. Creating order around yourself is one way in which you can try to exercise control and regain a sense of calm. But if we don't do that, what is the impact? How does clutter and untidiness make us feel emotionally? If you need the impetus to get tidying, it helps to understand the negative effect of clutter on your well-being. You might be surprised.

Do you find yourself looking around at your clutter and feeling overwhelmed? Perhaps it's a shelf full of knick-knacks that you don't even like. For lots of us, it's a pile of paper admin that topples over every time you accidentally touch it. Unless you're someone who thrives on disorder, clutter most likely leaves you feeling drained. Your external space reflects your inner state – if your brain is like a bedroom floor strewn with dirty laundry, are you going to be able to go out and tackle the world calmly and effectively?

Clutter makes it difficult to navigate life both physically and emotionally. You may find yourself feeling anxious, helpless, out of control, overwhelmed, drained and generally like your life force is being sucked out of you!

These aren't exaggerations. Worst of all, it is a vicious cycle – while you're paralyzed by the thought of all the clutter around you, it just keeps on accumulating. Let's be honest, clutter can be a source of great stress in our lives, and we're very good at trying to ignore it.

Psychologists believe that clutter has a huge effect on mental well-being. Studies have shown that it affects our ability to function and to think. Too much flying around in our brains or in our living spaces has an impact on our physical and mental health, our cognitive abilities and our overall sense of satisfaction with life. Because we identify so closely with our home environments, if that environment is messy, it makes the time we spend there less pleasurable. Psychologists think of 'home' not just as your physical environment but your whole 'lifeworld'. The more clutter you have, the harder it is to live comfortably in that lifeworld, and to navigate your way through it with a sense of happiness. What do psychologists suggest for combatting this? Streamlining and decluttering.

The good news is that clutter and mess are relatively easy to sort out. It may not feel like that when you think about what needs doing, but with a plan, you can tackle it, and wow, what a difference you'll feel.

If you're procrastinating about tidying, the task is only going to become more and more overwhelming. You'll feel increasingly distressed and dysfunctional within the environment – your home – which is supposed to be your place to retreat to in comfort.

But don't beat yourself up. It's important to realize that clutter is normal. Everyone accumulates possessions – it's part of the way we build a sense of ourselves and a 'home' around us. Likewise, we're all guilty of accumulating things in our lives that aren't possessions. Think about the friends you have who are toxic and exert a negative energy in your life. Do you accept every invitation you receive in fear of missing out, and end up exhausted and with no time to yourself? For your sanity's sake, there are all kinds of areas in your life that can benefit from being tidied up. And if you need any more convincing, the next chapter tells you all about the benefits of tackling your life with a feather duster and a trash bag ...

Of course, everyone is different and has a different response to clutter. Only you know how clutter makes you feel. You might even have a different response depending on the type of clutter. While a coffee table strewn with magazines and junk mail may send you spiralling into hell, you could find your higgledy-piggledy book reading corner absolute heaven. Both responses are okay! How you organize your life should be based on what makes you comfortable, content and happy. It's up to you to think carefully about what works for you – and of course, identify what isn't working and fix it.

Clutter smothers.
Simplicity breathes.

TERRI GUILLEMETS

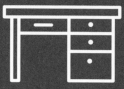

the benefits of being tidy

If the previous chapter has made you stop and think about why you have clutter, this chapter will galvanize you into activity. Realizing how clutter makes you feel physically and mentally is initially overwhelming. Perhaps you feel you lack the energy needed to make changes. Is it easiest just to let things carry on as they are? No! Not for your long-term well-being. Let's look at the flipside – the benefits of decluttering. These will give you the motivation and strength to create the inner calm you deserve.

Boost your energy

Rather than sitting looking glumly at the mess around you, stand up and tidy up. Even taking 5 minutes to tackle a disorganized desk in the middle of your working day can invigorate you. Throw away the trash, file the documents you've let stack up and give your email inbox a spring clean. You'll discover the tasks that have been looming over you for weeks are easily fixed in a matter of minutes. This sense of satisfaction will give you energy for the rest of the day. And as you ride high on that wave of achievement, you'll also find yourself motivated to extend that decluttering and organizing into more areas of your life. There's no stopping you now!

Clarity of values

Values are incredibly important as they define your personality. They support the way you behave and the habits you have, and allow you to navigate your life feeling happy and productive. Having excessive clutter or too much going on in your life has a negative impact on the clarity of your values. With that lack of clarity comes a feeling of paralysis – you don't know how to move things forward, and your creativity and productivity levels drop. As much as you want to organize your life and get back on track, you simply don't have the energy to do it. Take a step back. Contemplating what's in your life gives a real sense of what is and isn't important to you. Tidying, decluttering and organizing will clear out those things that don't matter, and leave you with those that do. What remains will help you to redefine your values and restore that all-important vision of who you are.

Peace of mind and harmony

A tidy space just begs you to relax. You can't do this if you're pushing aside the detritus of your life just to be able to find a space on your couch! Peace of mind means you're in sync with your emotions. You're able to stay calm in the face of stress, and be unshaken rather than overcome by anxiety. You've found your inner harmony. When you've tidied up the distractions and stress that come with being disorganized, your mind is left with the space to be calm and peaceful. Ommmmmm ....

Fight depression

If you're living with depression, organizing and decluttering can help you fight back. One small step a day – opening the mail from yesterday for example – can boost your self-confidence and self-esteem. It lets you get back the sense of self-worth. If you can lighten the load in your physical environment by removing things that are contributing to your stress (for example, a messy bedroom that stops you getting a good night's sleep), it will reduce the weight on your mind. Would freeing up your unnecessarily busy diary give you more time to focus on your own needs? Your mental well-being is paramount. Living a tidy, clutter-free life isn't a 'cure' for depression, but it should certainly be in your toolbox for getting your life back.

Cleaner air

We hear a lot about the emotional benefits of decluttering, but have you thought about how it benefits your physical environment? A tidy home can improve the air quality around you. Just think of all the ornaments and piles of junk that are accumulating dust. They're contributing to the toxins floating through the air and finding their way in to your lungs. You might find you're coughing or have irritated eyes. Any asthma sufferers in your household will find clutter particularly troublesome. If you can clear, clean or reorganize the dust magnets in your home, it's a big step towards breathing more easily and far healthier living.

Save time!

If you know where everything is, just think of the time you could save ... and the stress you could spare yourself. Sadly, this doesn't happen by itself and you need to put the work in. But if you can get organized, you'll wonder why you didn't do it sooner. It's not just about saving on stress – if you can get things done more quickly, just think of the time you can free up to spend doing something you love.

Reduces stress – what's not to like about that?

If you can minimize stress in your everyday life (or learn to deal with it better), you can reduce the risk of heart disease, high blood pressure and diabetes. It will ensure that your digestive, reproductive and immune systems function properly, and reduce symptoms of stress such as headaches and chest pain. If you're conscious that your clutter is a source of stress to you, get sorting it! The benefits to your health are undeniable. Of course, we face stress every day, but achieving peace of mind within your environment means you can better deal with it when it does come at you with a battering ram.

Material possessions: the more you own, the more they own you.

H.I. PHILLIPS

why saying goodbye is hard to do

Letting go is one of the hardest things to do when you're trying to declutter. You start off with great intentions to fill a bag for the thrift store but end up with only one thing in it. That trip to the thrift store never gets made, and you find yourself back at square one. There are all kinds of excuses – some personal – that we make for not parting with our possessions. We know that it's in our best interests but we just... can't... say... goodbye. Why are we our own worst enemies?

Your identity

It's not the things with monetary value or functional use that we find hardest to say goodbye to. The things we hate to part with are those that we see as an extension of ourselves. They're not what we own, they represent who we are. On a psychological level, it links to our sense of self-worth. If how you look is important to you, you'll find it incredibly hard to part with clothes, for example. If your sense of worth is tied up in your academic achievements, disposing of that pile of old school work is going to be heart-wrenching. Getting rid of things that represent our identity (and gain us approval from others) threatens our sense of self-worth. It can cause great sadness which in your own mind is akin to grief.

Nostalgia

Possessions that have memories attached can be particularly hard to say goodbye to. Reminiscing about the past creates all kinds of warm feelings, and makes us feel connected to other people. Our brains are hardwired to believe that the past was better than the present – that's why when we're feeling down, we're prone to be more nostalgic, pining for the 'good old days'. Items with memories – such as photographs and souvenirs – are what provide that ticket back to the past where we feel more secure. The best way to approach this is to reorient your mindset. Bring yourself back to the present, and also look to the future. Ask yourself whether the world would fall apart without these possessions. Memories remain in our heads regardless.

For tips on how to tidy and organize memories painlessly, see page 66.

Keep the end result in mind

There's no easy answer to tidying your life pain-free. For some, it will be immensely liberating every step of the way, but you may find yourself trudging unhappily through it. Keep the big picture in mind. Why are you doing this? What does the end result look like? Weigh up what is worse – a temporary feeling of sadness or an ongoing annoyance at the clutter interfering in your life. Focus on the trophy: a more organized home and life, a greater sense of clarity and a calmer, more resilient mind.

How many things are there which I do not want?

SOCRATES

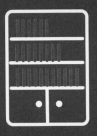

tidy, declutter or reorganize?

It's very tempting to think that being tidy is all about minimalism, and that to achieve this you need to dispose of everything. The idea is that having fewer possessions around you will be reflected in a clutter-free mind.
It's certainly true to a degree, but tidiness isn't simply about having fewer possessions. It's about finding a way of living that restores your sense of calm, and removes disruptions to harmony in your environment. The good news is that you have options: tidy, declutter or reorganize.

Tidy

Tidying is pretty much the umbrella of everything. To tidy can mean to place things neatly – think of a pile of magazines in a neat tower rather than strewn across the table – a massive improvement but nothing has been thrown away. Tidying can mean putting things back in their home, for example putting the laundry away into your closet. Tidying up might be what you do with your garden: pruning and clearing. Rather than being solely about reducing, tidying is about straightening up and having things in their place. In other words, it's taking control of your environment and your life, and not letting it control you.

If you think of tidying in that way, it makes it much less daunting. No one is expecting you to discard every last remnant of your existence and live in a cold, echoing shell of a home. And no one is going to wrench your prized possessions from your hands! What you're aiming for is harmony in your life, and a way to balance order and chaos.

Declutter

Decluttering has nowadays come to mean something quite radical – basically getting rid of everything you don't need. Or, as decluttering guru Marie Kondo suggests, anything that doesn't bring you joy. The word 'clutter' itself suggests things that are unnecessary and undesirable. If you think of tidying as putting things in order, decluttering is what you might need to do before you reach the tidying stage. Perhaps you have so much 'stuff' that there's no room to give everything the home it (and you) deserves. Decluttering therefore involves an element of disposal and an element of tidying. You're aiming to reduce the distractions around you, and then order (tidy) what's left to create an environment in which you feel calm and comfortable.

Decluttering can be as extreme or as gentle as you like. Again, it's what works best for you in terms of the environment you want to create. Perhaps you want to chuck everything in a bin and embrace the bare minimum – that could be exactly the head space you need (although please see page 78 for recycling and upcycling tips first!). Your goal might simply be to empty your kitchen of all the well-intentioned gadgets you never use and store them in the garage. Either way, decluttering is the perfect way to reinstate control over your life.

Reorganizing

Like tidying, reorganizing is all about rearranging things in a more pleasing way. It's not just changing the order of your trinkets on the shelf, of course – think of it as ordering your life so that it becomes more efficient and less stress-inducing. For example, do you waste time retrieving saucepans from the back of a cupboard when, as they're the ones you use more frequently, it would make better sense to store them at the front? It could be that your admin system is an absolute nightmare and has you waking up in cold sweats – yet the solution could be as simple as buying some lever-arch files and dividers. If you can make something better organized, it will become simpler and less stressful (just think of getting your kids out the door). Reorganizing doesn't necessarily involve throwing things away (although some would argue that owning less is better than organizing more). Take a step back and think hard about how you could do things in a better, more efficient way, and then implement that. The results in terms of stress and time-saving will be nothing short of amazing. Trust us!

In short, it's up to you to choose the approach you take to tidying your life and your space. You need to find whatever level of tidying/decluttering/reorganizing works for you and you feel comfortable with. Don't forget that you can extend that comfort zone further when you get better at putting order into your life. Who knows, you may discover you're a closet minimalist and feel cosiest in a room with the bare minimum of possessions. In your quest for a calmer self, the important thing is to keep firmly in mind that the benefits outweigh the somewhat painful process.

Being clear of clutter is one of the greatest aids I know to manifesting the life you want, and it is absolutely essential if you truly want to know joy and happiness in your life.

KAREN KINGSTON

how to get started

What obstacles do you need to overcome to start organizing and tidying your home and life? Perhaps it's time, or the sheer scale of the task that you need to address. You might be someone who finds it exceedingly hard to part with possessions. Or maybe you just simply don't know where to start. Read on for some great tips to get you on the road to a tidier, calmer life.

10 classic excuses

Do any of these excuses sound familiar?

But I might need it/use it/wear it one day.

It's got too many memories.

It was expensive.

It's wasteful just to get rid of stuff.

I don't have a home for it so I'll just leave it here.

It's too hard so why bother starting?

It was a gift.

My children might want it one day.

I don't have the time.

I'm going to fix it.

Remember that decluttering doesn't necessarily mean things have to go in the bin. They can be regifted, recycled, upcycled or simply reorganized.

What does tidy mean to you?

Before you get started, take a moment to think about what tidiness means to you. Remember that you're doing this for your own calmness and clarity, so don't try to meet other people's standards – it has to be what is life-enhancing for you. It could be a whole reorganization of your home, or it could be something as small as opening the post and recycling/filing it every day. If you can feel it making a difference to your life and your headspace, then it's working.

Set realistic goals

Time, energy, emotional state, support – these should all be factored in when deciding what your goals for tidying are. It's great to be ambitious, but if it's too ambitious, you may find yourself feeling overwhelmed before you even get started. Break down the bigger jobs into smaller tasks that you can conquer, and tick off one at a time. (To-do lists are awesome – see below.) As well as setting realistic goals, make sure you're working to a realistic timescale. Give yourself plenty of time, and if it does take longer, don't beat yourself up about it.

Write an on-point to-do list

Everyone has their own techniques for writing a to-do list. However, what should you consider if you want to create a productive to-do list that actually gets things done?

Only have one list. It's easier to have everything in once place, and that way you can also prioritize items.

•

Prioritizing is important. What do you want to do first? Do you want to tackle the biggest job that will make the biggest difference to your life? Or do you want to tick off the smaller items first to clear your time for the big stuff? Just beware of doing the small things first as a way of avoiding the bigger jobs.

•

Write everything down, no matter how insignificant. It's a great way to create space in your mind, as the list replaces relying on your brain to remind you of what needs doing.

•

Only write down things that can be completed and ticked off. E.g. 'Clean the bathroom' rather than 'Live happily ever after'!

•

Rewrite the list each day so it only includes the things left to do. Basically, declutter your to-do list. You can still enjoy crossing off tasks with a big, fat, neon highlighter pen each day!

Make the time

Finding time to get things done is a big obstacle in everyone's life. As much as we long do something, everyday life and routine often eat away at the time we've ring fenced. It's a pretty sound excuse, but there are ways to reclaim your time.

Declutter your schedule (more of this on page 69!). Is it really necessary to go to Bob from Accounts' leaving drinks when you've only spoken to him once (via email)? Along with this comes learning to say 'no' (see page 71).

Rethink your routine. Maybe you've spent the last five years slumped on the couch watching box sets after dinner. What are you really getting out of it? If you've slipped into something through habit, change that routine and free up the time for doing something else.

Cut out distractions. These days, for many of us that means exiting the internet and putting down our smartphone.

Prioritize. If tidying your kitchen cupboards is a higher priority than putting your books in order of color, leave the literary rainbow until another day.

Remember – if you've broken down the jobs that need doing, grabbing even just 5 minutes to do something small can be productive. You don't have to complete a day's worth of decluttering to make a positive difference.

Find the motivation

As big as the task may seem, try and visualize the endpoint. It may be a long tunnel, but the light at the end of it will bring real benefits to your physical and mental well-being. Use positive visualization to imagine yourself living free of clutter and with more time to enjoy the things you love. These are achievable goals, provided you approach them methodically. If you need more incentives, think about how you could reward yourself along the way. Treat yourself to some new season clothes if you successfully streamline your closet. Buy a new vacuum when you've finally cleared the floorspace if that floats your boat. Really, bribing yourself is okay in these circumstances!

Adopt a new attitude

Tidying definitely needs a 'can do' attitude, and that can be hard if you're feeling overwhelmed, anxious or hopeless. This is another reason why breaking the job down into smaller portions is so important. It's far easier to challenge yourself to conquer a small task yet the satisfaction is still high. Every task ticked off will see your confidence grow. You may even start to enjoy yourself. The next job will be that little bit easier than the last, and before you know it, you'll be feeling a world of difference. Even if you find it hard to start off with a 'positive mental attitude', it will grow. And, if you're starting from a low point, cultivating that attitude is one of the goals of the process.

Clutter makes life complicated, heavy and wearisome. Simplicity makes life relaxed, carefree and invigorating.

TOMMY NEWBERRY

the 4-box challenge

You now know what you need to do to get started on the road to a calmer you. Just apply everything in the previous chapters and you'll be good to go. You've got the motivation, time, goals and to-do list - what more could you possibly need? Boxes. Or bags. But preferably boxes if you're trying to be neat and orderly – this is the new you after all! Boxes are your way of organizing what you're organizing (are you still following?) so that you don't just end up with a pile of random things spilling across your floor.

Why 4 boxes?

Each box has a specific purpose, and is designed to focus your mind and organize your output.

1. Donate

This box is the home for anything that you don't need, but is in good enough condition to be given away. It could find a new home with a friend or family member, or via a thrift store or rummage sale.

2. Store

If you have something you don't want to throw away (perhaps it's something you only use at Christmas time), declutter and free up some valuable space by storing it in a marked box in a garage or attic.

3. Sell

Whether you're planning to sell online or have a garage sale, this is the box for items that could make you some money. (Just resist the urge to let the box fester somewhere without ever actually selling the contents!)

4. Throw away/recycle

There will always be items that you can't donate, store or sell, so this is your trash box. Do check though whether anything can be recycled rather than simply become part of our ever-growing landfill problem.

Question everything!

Each item you use or own ask yourself:

Do I use this?

Do I have more than one of these?

Would I buy it again?

Does it really make me like it better?

Don't love it?

These questions will help you decide whether it earns a home in your cottage or not. Be ruthless... surrounding ... only with things you really love and that really make a ...

...

Don't dilly dally

You've got to grab hold of things firmly when you find you're moving. A lot of the best stores you can be buried and borrow. Take the practical and sentimental ...

...

if you can't stand the heat ...

... get out of the kitchen. Or, take a more rationale approach and tidy it. Kitchens are predominantly cupboards and workspace, and both accumulate clutter more quickly than you can say 'spaghetti carbonara'. It's the part of the house where people tend to pass through and also congregate more regularly, leaving detritus in their wake. How often have you parked something on the counter for convenience and then weeks later it's still there (probably underneath something else by that time)? We're all guilty of it. It's time to reclaim your kitchen!

Getting started

Grab your boxes. Set a timer – don't try to tackle the whole kitchen in one sitting or you'll set yourself up to fail. Start with 30 minutes and really – and we mean REALLY – focus. Decluttering at random will leave you feeling like you've made no impact whatsoever. Attempt just one drawer or cupboard at a time and really crack it.

Create efficient cupboard space

Shutting a cupboard door to hide the contents is a fantastic way to make your kitchen look tidy. But what happens when you open it? Do things fall out? Can you find what you need? If your kitchen needs decluttering, the answers to the last two questions will be a resounding 'Yes!' and 'No!'. What you need are efficient cupboards that are designed for using, not just storing.

Make more space. Unfortunately, you can't grow the size of your cabinets. Remove what you no longer need and dispose of food that's out of date. Once you've pared back the contents, you'll be surprised how much extra room there is. Don't be tempted to fill every inch – remember, the idea is to make it less stressful trying to find and retrieve things.

Store items logically. You want dried pasta. You want tinned tomatoes. Does that mean walking from one side of the kitchen to the other? Think of the time you could save if you stored things logically; if, for example, the sugar for your coffee was in the same cupboard as the coffee granules you'd have more time for drinking and enjoying that coffee. Consider what items in your kitchen sit naturally together. You may find that this evolves gradually as you start to mindfully use the space, but logical storage will eventually fall into place.

Invest in some clever time – and space-saving gadgets. It's all well and good having less in your cupboards, but the fact remains that anything on a top shelf or that gets pushed to the back becomes hard to find. If you search online or visit your local hardware shop, you'll find devices to make your life a little easier. Pull-out baskets and carousels are a great way to get to things at the back of cupboards and make use of otherwise dead space. Stepped stands make it simple to see what's lurking at the back of a cupboard by lifting items into view.

Storage

Clear containers are great to use in the kitchen. Not only can you see what's in them (so no more taking ten bags out of the cupboard before you find what you want) but they're also easily stackable. If you're fed up of packets slipping and sliding around your cupboards, stacking lovely straight-sided, flat-bottomed containers could be the key to your serenity. One warning though – storage containers do have the tendency to multiply and lose their lids. When decluttering your kitchen, only keep those containers that still have a matching lid. This saves on a lot of annoyance.

Create zones

What's the best way to organize a kitchen? As with storing things logically, creating zones within your kitchen is a great way to increase efficiency and reduce your stress. Don't worry – you don't have to refit your kitchen; it's more about having things close together that you might need at the same time. For example, your collection of wooden spoons is best placed next to the oven top. Obvious really!

Experts suggest the following 'zones':

Consumables – all your food in one place.

Non-consumables – plates, dishes, cups, glasses, cutlery, etc.

Cleaning – usually the area around the sink.

Preparation – usually a counter area with chopping board, knives, etc, to hand.

Cooking – the area around your oven and oven top.

Implementing zones in this way should mean you spend less time dashing back and forth with your temperature rising faster than a pan of peas.

Under the sink

The place where everything cleaning-related gets deposited – cloths, sponges, the spray cleaner that didn't perform as promised but you've never thrown away. Look underneath everyone's sink and you'll find the same. So, get decluttering those cleaning supplies. There are few things more annoying than trying to reach a bottle at the back and all the bottles at the front tumbling out like bowling pins. You should be able to move serenely through your kitchen space!

What is your kitchen for?

This is not as obvious a question as you might think. Of course, it's used for cooking and eating, but have you thought what else? A drop spot for your children's school bags and somewhere for them to do their homework? A resting place for piles of post and unfiled admin? And more besides, no doubt. If you want to keep your kitchen (and your brain) clutter-free, you need to consider how to manage this going forward. Your kitchen is exactly that – a kitchen – so additional activities shouldn't disrupt its primary use. Free up a drawer where you can store pens and pencils, keeping them close at hand for homework time rather than rolling all over your counter top. Find a new home for incoming post, or at least find something suitable to keep it contained in.

Need more persuasion?

The benefits of a tidy kitchen are too good to ignore:

Clutter-free counter tops are so much easier and quicker to clean.

•

Studies have shown that a tidy kitchen encourages healthier eating.

•

By using your kitchen more efficiently, you'll be running around less, saving time and your sanity.

•

Spend just 10 minutes at the end of each day tidying up any annoying clutter that's crept in, and you'll be well on your way to maintaining a calm and productive kitchen.

A place for everything, and everything in its place.

MRS BEETON

a peaceful bathroom

Bathrooms can be a place for quiet contemplation. An oasis where you can lie back in bubbles and soak your worries away. But what if it's not? What if one of the few places where you can justifiably shut the door on the world is packed with clutter, and makes you want to reach for the wine rather than the bubble bath? Thankfully, what's usually one of the smallest rooms in the home can be one of the easiest to tackle. Goodbye chaos, hello sanctuary.

As with all rooms in your home, tidying your bathroom is all about organization. What's most challenging is that your bathroom is one of the places where you're most likely to find smaller items and things that end up half-used – think make-up and medicines. Not forgetting the bottles of toiletries that drive you to distraction because they JUST WON'T STAY STANDING UP!!! Let's get started ...

The medicine cabinet

A well-stocked medicine cabinet brings peace of mind as it means you're well-prepared for what life throws at you. But it can also be a hot bed of clutter. Go through each item and remove anything that has gone out-of-date. (Your local drugstore may accept out of date drugs for disposal.) Make a list of anything crucial that you need to replace. It's one of the few places where it's okay to store items 'just in case', so don't worry if you don't end up reducing quantities. What's important for your peace of mind is that you know you have everything you might need and that it's useable – no more panicked late-night trips to a drugstore.

Get clever with organization

If you open a drawer in your bathroom and it's swimming with bottles, tissues, hairbands, tweezers and the like, you need to get clever. Tray organizers are a perfect way to compartmentalize items and stop them turning into an infuriating jumble. Aim to keep the items you use every day easily accessible and visible. Your bathroom is a big part of how you start your day, so start it well by not getting stressed hunting for what you need.

More brilliant bathroom organizational hacks:

A magnetic strip fixed inside a cabinet door is a great way to organize the small items like hair grips and tweezers which can be impossible to find.

●

As long as you can resist filling them with clutter, shelves are a good way to free up surface space. They're also the solution to that annoying row of shampoos and shower gels that inevitably builds up along the side of your bath.

•

You can (almost) never have too many hooks in your bathroom, especially for towels. Hooks are also great inside cupboards for smaller items that get more easily lost.

•

They hold so much promise, but avoid suction cups for hanging items! In a steamy bathroom environment, they will eventually detach, and you'll be left with more mess than you started with.

Bath toy nasties

Mould. Mildew. Not what you want on your kids' bath toys. If you're worried about the cleanliness of what's sharing the bathwater – or just can't stand looking at mouldy plastic any longer – it's time to get rid of the nasties. Either pop the toys in the dishwasher, soak them in sterilizing tablets, or soak them overnight in a white vinegar mix (225 ml per 5 litres of warm water). Any that don't come clean should be consigned to the trash or recycled. Now, you can stop panicking when a toy goes near your child's mouth.

Get your rubber gloves on

There's nothing more therapeutic than rolling up your sleeves and getting busy cleaning. Seeing before and after results is immensely satisfying, and gives you a reason to feel very pleased with yourself. Bathrooms are particularly good at getting grimy and hairy. Make a list of any cleaning products you need, and then attack everything that's been niggling at you for months. (Need we say dirty grouting?) A deep cleaned, sparkly bathroom will give you a wonderful sense of calm and renewed sense of energy.

Create a haven

Once you've dealt with the grime and the clutter, the fun can start. This is the bit that really focuses on the calmer you that you're seeking. Think about what makes you feel relaxed and what will help you enjoy your bathroom more.

Scented candles to set the mood for chilling in the bath.

•

A radio – upbeat music while you brush your teeth in the morning sets you up for a great start to the day.

•

Artwork – the bathroom isn't where most people think about displaying art, but why not?!

•

A stool next to your bath – perfect for holding your book and glass of wine.

•

Add a plant that loves a humid atmosphere – even better if it's one with air purifying qualities too.

Be careless in your dress if you must, but keep a tidy soul.

MARK TWAIN

wardrobes and
floordrobes

Your bedroom: the place where you're supposed to
sleep deeply, wake gently and have wonderful dreams.
Sadly, this isn't always the case. It's a room that's often
prone to becoming a dumping ground away from
prying eyes. It's tempting not to tackle your bedroom
as it's usually only you (and your partner who no doubt
contributes to the mess) that sees it. Yet if you want
to restore calm to your mind in both your sleeping and
waking hours, a tidy and hygienic bedroom is vitally
important. It needs to be your place of escape, and not
a never-ending source of stress.

Get a good night's sleep

FACT. A clean and tidy bedroom equals a better night's sleep. Consider the evidence:

In 2015, a study in the US found that people with cluttered bedrooms who were prone to hoarding were more likely to find it harder to get to sleep and experience disturbed sleep.

•

In the UK, 44% of adults suffer from an allergy, and 59% of indoor allergy sufferers say that their symptoms get worse in the bedroom.

•

A survey by the National Sleep Foundation in the US found that people who made their bed every day were 19% more likely to get a good night's sleep. (And 75% said they slept better with fresh sheets.)

Tackling the last two points is straightforward and takes very little time. Regularly dust and vacuum surfaces and floors, vacuum your mattress to remove dust and leave it to air, and wash all of your bedding thoroughly. These simple steps instantly give you the cleaner, dust-free air that's so important for a good night's sleep.

Clutter-free sleep

Before you deep clean, you'll need to declutter. Start with the dreaded floordrobe – that untidy heap of clothing that gets discarded on the floor. Put it away! Or put it in the laundry basket. Either way, when it's on your floor, you'll either trip over it or not be able to find it when you need it. Get into the good habit of not using your floor as closet space.

Given the importance of a clean bedroom, aim to reduce the number of dust-gathering knick-knacks you have. Keeping surfaces as clear as you can helps cut down the time it takes you to clean and make your surroundings more soothing on the eye (think a beautiful country landscape rather than an industrial one). Don't feel that you need to go completely minimal though – a few well-placed items that you find beautiful or that evoke warm memories should have a place in your sanctuary.

Are you making full use of storage solutions in your bedroom? Not only does getting organized clear your headspace, it makes it easier to find things. If you're short of drawer and wardrobe space, get clever with the space under the bed. It doesn't have to be where you consign things to gather dust – simple storage boxes slotted under the bed are a great way to keep items out of sight but still easily accessible. Blanket boxes and trunks are also perfect for stashing away clothes, bedding and towels.

From the floordrobe to wardrobe

Decluttering your wardrobe is a topic that's warranted books all of its own! Our clothes are so integral to our identity, no wonder it's so hard not to hang on to everything. It's an area where you must be truly ruthless and not think too hard about what you're doing. It's tricky, but it's an incredible way to restore calm and clarity in your mind.

Top ten golden rules of wardrobe vacuum decluttering

1. Start by taking everything out, with the idea of only putting back in what you want to keep.

2. Throw away (or take to a cloth recycling facility) any clothing that's ripped beyond repair, stained and can't be saved, or threadbare.

3. Set aside anything that you don't want but can resell or donate to charity.

4. Collect together anything that needs fixing – and make sure you get round to doing it so you can start wearing them again.

5. Have you worn the item in the last year? If not, don't keep it. Despite any 'what if?' scenarios you conjure up it's highly unlikely you will wear it.

6. Do you actually like it? If you're keeping something because it's the height of fashion and you're 'supposed' to like it, that's not a good reason. Only keep what you like and enjoy wearing.

7. Don't keep something that doesn't fit just because it might fit one day. Has that ever happened?! Worst case scenario, you can always buy it again at a later date.

8. If you have clothes that you only ever wear on holiday (that string bikini probably doesn't work at your local public pool), stash them away for when you need

them. They don't need to be fighting for space in your wardrobe with all the clothes you wear regularly.

9. When everything you want to keep is back in your wardrobe/drawers, make sure that it's all organized neatly and is visible. You're more likely to wear what you can see and find.

10. Focus on the big picture. If you think too much about the negatives, you'll miss out on the positive outcome you're aiming for – a tidy wardrobe full of clothes you love and can find! Don't get bogged down by little details.

Declutter your décor

If you want to really overhaul your bedroom space, why not reward your decluttering effort with a refresh of the décor? There are simple changes you can make to create a greater feeling of calm.

Start with color. The most soothing bedroom colors are lavender, light gray, soft green, pale blue and deep blue. These colors encourage a cozy and calm ambience, reduce stress and anxiety and promote relaxation.

Do you like patterns? Thankfully, there's no need to avoid them in a seriously soothing bedroom. Do use them carefully though – remember that small patterns look best on small things like lampshades, and large patterns work better on larger things (e.g. duvet covers). Follow these simple rules, and your décor will make your room feel less cluttered and infinitely more relaxing.

You can't reach for anything new if your hands are still full of yesterday's junk.

LOUISE SMITH

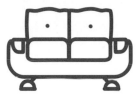

a living room for living in

As homes become increasingly open plan, it's very hard to shut a door on an untidy room. Your living room is your place to flop down in at the end of a busy day. What you don't want is to have to clear a space every time you sit on the vacuum or to be distracted from a movie by the pile of papers teetering on the edge of the coffee table. You'll never be able to savor the calm. When tidying your living room, keep in mind an image of the room you want to see when you're lying back on the couch relaxing with a glass of wine!

Get sorted

It's back to the 4-box challenge (see page 33)! Starting with items you can see, work your way through deciding what you can discard, sell, donate or store elsewhere. There's no need to keep that broken lamp unless you really think you're going to fix it. Just getting your living room to the visibly tidy stage gives you the right to pat yourself on the back. Step back and savor how good it feels. It's not an easy task, but seeing positive results will spur you to go beyond your comfort zone and move one step closer to your calm zone.

Not having a place for things to 'live' can be a real bug bear – you put them somewhere with the best intentions, but there they stay while you get increasingly irritated by them. If you can't move them to where they rightly belong in another room, create additional, tidy storage. A magazine rack can quickly clear a table top of papers and catalogs (as can a recycling bin!). The growing pile of DVDs next to the TV will stop toppling over if you put it in a basket. Sorting these small annoyances is a quick and easy way to de-stress.

Furniture and accessories

Having too much furniture in your living room can contribute to a feeling of claustrophobia – as if your room is controlling you rather than vice versa. Think about how you use your room like with your clothes, if you're not using furniture or don't like it, why keep it? You might feel obliged to keep the armchair you inherited from Great Aunt Mavis, but if it takes up too much space and you feel no joy in it then donate it to charity – someone else is bound to love it.

Make your furniture work doubly hard. For example, an ottoman can work as storage, extra seating and a table. Think outside the box a little (no pun intended!).

•

Move your bulkiest furniture away from the entrance to your living room, ideally to the wall that's furthest away from the door. This creates a real sense of space as you enter the room, letting you feel like you're the one in control and not being overwhelmed by furniture.

Rearrange your couch and chairs so they're facing each other. This encourages chatting and interaction and makes for a happier, more relaxed space.

Place a mirror on the wall opposite a window or door to create the illusion of more space. Let as much light in to the room as you can. Natural light provides a wonderful mood boost.

Throws can be used to disguise your less-than-perfect couch and armchairs, and to add a pop of calming color to your living room. They're also marvellous for cozying up under and relaxing.

Add a plant to your living space. Caring for plants is very calming, and you'll cultivate your compassionate side. It's even more calming if there's little danger of you killing the plant, so choose something easy to care for like a snake plant or aloe vera.

Taming the toys

If your kids' bedrooms are full to the brim and you don't have a playroom, where do the excess toys end up? Most likely your living room. There are ways to manage this so that you don't end up swamped by teddies or treading on rogue Lego pieces.

Storage is key. If you're short of space, a shelving unit that holds boxes or trays is a great way to organize toys. As long as you can put their clutter into boxes quickly at the end of day and store it out of sight, your serenity is guaranteed.

Having fewer toys encourages your children to be more creative, so implement a plan of attack:

Work with your kids to decide what stays and what can be donated to charity or to another family. Of course, they'll want to keep everything you don't, so encourage them to sell things too – a little extra in the money box is a great incentive.

•

Broken or items missing pieces – these go, no question.

•

If there are toys that haven't been played with for a long time, put them in a box and store them somewhere out of the way (such as a garage or attic). If your kids don't ask for them in the next three months, they're safe to eliminate from your home.

•

Remember, not all the toys your children own need to be out at once. Think about rotating them – some out, some in storage. Not only does this reduce the clutter, it stops your kids getting bored of the same toys.

Set peace of mind
as your highest goal,
and organize your life
around it.

BRIAN TRACY

create a calm workspace

Working from home is full of distractions at the best of times. Whether it's laundry that needs doing, neighbors calling by for a chat or something fascinating on the radio, it can be hard to focus. A cluttered workspace is the icing on the cake. The state of your desk in the office can also have a negative effect on your stress levels. What can you do to create a serene workspace that encourages you to stop procrastinating and get things done? They don't say that a tidy desk is a tidy mind for nothing!

Paper, paper everywhere

In theory, the more we do online the less paper we should be printing out. Sadly, that's far from the truth. Desks are like a magnet to paper – mailshots, invoices, to-do lists. If you can't find your stapler for the mound of paper, this is the first place to start.

File it. And if you don't have a filing system, now's the time to create one. You don't need a filing cabinet – a simple lever-arch file with dividers will do. And if organizing and categorizing is your thing, you'll find creating a filing system immensely satisfying.

●

Have a tray on your desk for any items that need actioning. Worrying that you've forgotten to do something is very stressful, so make sure the important stuff doesn't get lost under a paper mountain.

●

If it doesn't need filing or to take up space on your desk, recycle it. Tidy desk and saving the planet – two happy outcomes for the price of one!

The 'homely' desk

Your desk, especially in an office, is prone to become a home-from-home. Do you put up family photos, bring in trinkets or have a row of cuddly toys sitting on top of your monitor? This may make your desk your 'own' and create a comfort blanket, but it stops you from having a clear and focused mind. Remove anything from your desk that isn't essential to your day-to-day work. It will also make your desk a whole lot cleaner – the average desk is 400 times dirtier than the average toilet seat! Keep that in mind as you deep clean your desk with an antibacterial wipe.

Make drawers your friend. Don't think of it as hiding the clutter; drawers are a brilliant way to keep the things you need – staplers, paper clips, envelopes, etc – off your desk but still close to hand. The tidier your desk, the greater clarity you'll have to focus on the job at hand. With that clear mind comes calmness.

Embrace digital ...

Computers are 'naturally' brilliant at organizing things for you. If the clutter of your email inbox is making you tear your hair out, start filing emails into folders as they arrive, and flag those that need actioning. There are few things more stressful when sitting at your desk than seeing 20,000 emails staring at you. Get paper off your desk by scanning it and storing/filing it on your computer. Use your electronic calendar rather than a desk calendar – the bonus is that it will bleep alerts at you. Basically, let your computer do the hard work of storing and remembering things for you, freeing up your mind to focus.

... but beware of digital distractions!

Having too many things ringing, beeping or vibrating at you is not conducive to a calm mind. Especially if you're trying to focus on a piece of work, switch off notification pings on your computer and phone to remove the temptation of responding to every one. Are there 20 tabs open on your browser? Now there's a way to make your head explode. Close the ones you don't need as soon as you're finished with the page. Is social media tap-tap-tapping on your shoulder all the time? Resist the urge to constantly check your accounts. Set aside short chunks of time in your day for checking social media, allowing you to focus your mind on work when you need to. Flitting between digital distractions does little more than set your brain in a whirl and render you unable to focus on any one thing.

Make the end of the day the right start for the next

At the end of your working day, make sure you give your desk a final tidy. It only takes 5-10 minutes, and means that the next day you can sit down with a clear mind, ready to crack on.

Delete any emails from your inbox that you don't need to keep.

•

Rewrite your to-do list ready for the next day.

•

Do any filing to stop that paper mountain from rebuilding itself.

tidy up your finances

Money comes high up on most people's list of worries. It's easy to not feel in control of your finances, especially if numbers tend to leave you flummoxed. And that's even before you consider all the products and jargon that banks and financial services throw at you. While you might not ever become a financial expert, there are ways to tidy up your finances so that you can deal with them with a calmer mind. Ultimately, that means less worry. So, get ready to consolidate, simplify and save.

Budgeting

Knowing your outgoings and income are crucial to your peace of mind if you worry about money. If you have no idea and just hope for the best each month, you need to start organizing. A simple spreadsheet is actually all you need – list all your monthly outgoings (home, insurance, utility bills, food bill, memberships, taxes, etc.) and set that against how much money is coming in to your home. A straightforward sum will show you what money you have to spare. Keep a record of your spending on extras (clothes, going out, etc) so you can stay within your means.

And if there isn't any spare money, you now have a detailed breakdown of where you can look to cut down costs. Be ruthless about tidying your finances. If you can't afford that monthly magazine subscription, cancel it until you can.

Set goals and save

Having a budget fills many people with horror because they think it means no fun and no treats. That's not the case. Having a budget stops you worrying about spending too much, and allows you to plan better for the fun stuff. Set yourself goals – what do you want to save for? How can you do it? When the time to book a vacation comes, you'll know how much you have to spend, and won't be looking down the back of the couch for spare change! Manage your money clearly and calmly, and it won't be able to control you.

Spring clean the clutter

Finances generate oodles of paper admin. File all your important documents in one place – home details, insurance policies, car documents, etc – so that they're always to hand, and you're never panicking about finding them. Shred any out-of-date documents that you no longer need. If you receive paper bank statements, opt to receive them electronically and reduce your (and the planet's) paper mountain.

Tidy up your credit cards

Do you have ten different credit cards in your wallet? Chances are that you don't even use them all anymore. Consolidating cards will help you feel more in control. Cancel any that you don't use and that have a zero balance. Pay off any that you can, or transfer all your balances to one card. There are often good deals available for doing just that, and it will save you money.

Use comparison websites

It can be time-consuming to review all your finance providers, but if it saves you money and reduces stress levels, then it's time well spent. Online comparison sites are a great way to find the best deals on credit cards, bank accounts and home and car insurance with the minimum of fuss. It's easy to be lazy when we've set up our finances – a provider works out well so we just stick with them even when their prices go up. Shopping around and getting yourself the best deal is immensely satisfying, and puts you calmly back in the driving seat.

Stay on top of your finances. Don't leave that up to others.

LEIF GARRETT

organize your memories

Photographs

still have a drawer of photographs somewhere in your home. You'll set out with good intentions to ruthlessly sort the drawer, but three hours later, you'll be on a trip down memory lane. So, you need some rules! Discard any photos that are duplicates, unflattering, under/ overexposed, out of focus, have heads chopped off, are of people who hold bad memories and people you don't know. This should pare down your collection quite considerably.

A great idea is to scan your photos so that you can store them electronically. That way, you can also organize them neatly in folders to make them easy to find. It takes a bit of time but is well worth the effort.

Creating an album for the photos you consider particularly special is another way to consolidate and organize your collection. Follow the same rules as above, and only include the photos you really love.

Make a scrapbook

Are you forever finding old tickets that you've kept because they remind you of a great night out or vacation? If you really, REALLY can't part with them, at least get them organized. A simple scrapbook is the perfect was to save little bits and pieces that have sentimental value. It could be anything – tickets, leaflets, photos, menus, wrappers – although obviously ideally flat! Do remember just to include things you love, or you'll find yourself needing to buy a bigger home to store all your scrapbooks.

Children's artwork

If, like most, your children produce a constant stream of artwork, you're faced with a parent's biggest dilemma: (lovingly) keep or (heartlessly) throw away? When your kids have put so much effort in, it seems cruel to discard their masterpieces. Plus, art is a great way to remember the stages your kids went through. But you do need to start on the premise that you cannot keep it all. Pick out the highlights, the pieces you really love and that show a streak of genius or humor. You're keeping the best bits so there's no need to feel guilty. If you don't want to display any of the artwork, simply scan it and save it. There are even apps that can manage this for you.

When dealing with sentimental items, the thing to remember is that no one is asking you to purge your home completely. It's this attachment and nostalgia that makes us human. But what you can do is ensure they don't take an emotional toll on you. It is possible to strike a balance that stops you from being overwhelmed and allows you your peace of mind.

tidy your time

Are you doing too much? Are you busy doing everything for other people but nothing for you? Is your schedule so crammed that you can't find a pocket of calm in which to pause and restore your equilibrium? Decluttering your diary and how you use your time can help you focus on what matters to you. How you spend your time should bring you joy, and not feel like a chore. If it does feel like hard work, you need to rethink it and move on. As with tidying your home, approaching your time more mindfully is a wonderful way of reducing pressure and stress, and finding inner calm.

Time management

By following some basic rules, it's easy to organize your time better and break out of bad habits. The following can apply to all kinds of scenarios, whether it's preparing for a meeting or tackling the housework. Focus is a keyword!

1. Set goals
What do you need to do and by when? Focus on the task in hand and ignore what doesn't contribute to your goal.

2. Prioritize
Are you doing the most pressing job first? Don't procrastinate and find yourself just doing the easiest one. Is what you're doing contributing to a goal?

3. Learn when to say 'no'
If something doesn't contribute to your goal, it's okay to say no. (See below.)

4. Make a to-do list
Get it out of your head and onto paper. Tasks are more likely to get done if you write them down – fact!

5. Beware of distractions
Step away from the smartphone – or whatever your weak point is! Being distracted will make even the quickest job take forever. Focus on one thing at a time, ignore pings in your inbox and you'll get the job done with minimum stress.

6. Consolidate your calendars

Don't have a paper calendar running alongside an electronic calendar. That's a sure-fire way to make your head explode.

Saying 'no'

If instilling calmness in your life means staying in control, being able to say 'no' is vitally important. Finding your diary cluttered with things that you don't want or need to do can sap your energy and increase your stress levels. Saying 'no' isn't easy, so how can you do it without being rude?

Quite simply: use the word 'no'! Don't umm and ahh – say it confidently so that it's clear you mean it.

Give some explanation but keep it short.

Suggest an alternative – this can ease any tension, just make sure it's something you want to do!

If it's the case that you've simply got too much on but would otherwise have said yes, say that and postpone the date.

Make use of small pockets of time

While you shouldn't be trying to cram something in to every minute of the day, be organized about how you make use of small pockets of time. It could be while you're waiting for a pan to boil or when you're on your commute. Use this time to do something you love – read a book or an article – or do a short, calming meditation. If you're worrying about something, call a friend to chat, or make a to-do list to tackle your worry. Don't think of time used to de-stress as wasted time! Tidying up your life is all about freeing up time and headspace for YOU.

Finding time for you

At the center of everything talked about in this book is YOU. All the organizing you do, whether it's possessions, finances or time, is intended to make space in your life for you to enjoy. Throughout the process, you should hold in your mind a picture of what you're going to gain – increased serenity and less stress. The time you'll save is also an amazing reward, so think carefully about how you can use that time to cultivate your inner calm even further. Perhaps you'll decide to take up yoga or learn to meditate, rediscover an old hobby, take up painting or read all the books and watch all the films you've been wanting to. Taking time out from the pressures and busyness of life and focusing on YOU is where you'll find your calm inner self. Your well-being is a priority, so never feel guilty about making time for yourself.

Organising is what you do before you do something, so that when you do it, it is not all mixed up.

A. A. MILNE

spring clean your friends

Yes, this may sound ruthless but it's something we'd all like to do! As you get older, move through jobs or live in different neighborhoods, it's impossible not to accumulate acquaintances. And 'acquaintance' is the right word, because how many of these people would you actually count as genuine friends? To nurture our soul, we need to surround ourselves with people who are supportive, and bring us joy and comfort. You might feel that you need to be kind to everyone, but as you read at the end of the last chapter, sometimes you need to put your own well-being first.

Toxic friends

A 'toxic friend' is the exact opposite of what you'd expect from a friend – they don't have your interests at heart, they're selfish and rude, everything is about them, they compete with you, try to control you and criticize you – all in all, your friendship is an emotional rollercoaster. It's an incredibly stressful relationship to maintain and you may find yourself vulnerable to higher blood pressure, depression and anxiety as a result. A genuine friendship has a completely different effect, and studies have shown that having a solid and supportive friendship group can actually increase your life expectancy.

How to say goodbye for good

Once you've come to realize someone isn't healthy for you, how can you declutter them from your life as painlessly as possible?

It's hard to tell someone that you don't want them in your life anymore. Remember, you don't owe them a detailed explanation so keep it short and to the point. Be honest.

If you don't need to explicitly tell them you don't want to see them, you can simply gradually distance yourself. Keep yourself busy elsewhere with other friends and let time do the work.

Don't expect them to leave you alone immediately. After all, they believe they're a great friend! Distancing yourself may take time, so be patient and firm.

Block them on social media, your phone and email. Make it as hard for them to contact you as possible. Delete emails and social media posts that connect you.

•

Resist the urge to re-engage on any level. Whatever they might do and however angry it might make you feel, ignore it and let it wash over you.

Put yourself first

This is a hard thing to do when you're used to trying to please other people, but it needs to be done for your own physical and emotional well-being. Focus on the friends who bring stability and happiness to your life – the ones who love you for who you are. Reclaim all the time and energy you've been expending on toxic friends and channel it into the people whose friendships you truly value. With a trusted support network comes the security and calmness of mind that you deserve.

Social media

2,347 friends. Really?! How many of these are people you are actually interested in, rather than simply wanting to nose about in their lives? Social networking takes up an inordinate amount of time, sucks us into a vortex and then spits us out glassy eyed. If the amount of information appearing in your timeline is so vast that you miss what the people you really care about are saying, it's time to start clicking the 'unfriend' button. Reducing the stream of information that the digital age bombards you with can only bring your stress levels down.

Clutter is not just physical stuff. It's old ideas, toxic relationships and bad habits. It's anything that does not support your better self.

ELEANOR BROWN

recycle, repurpose and upcycle

It's all well and good removing items you no longer desire from your home, but items' goods to your planet, it ends up in landfill. While decluttering, be mindful of the waste before removing and it's faster and it's not for the planet. If you follow the 3-step challenge method... it you'll have a clear way of sorting where things should go next. Make, reuse, 'repurpose' and upcycle your belongings and enjoy the satisfaction of giving to others, saving money and the planet, and unleashing your creative side.

Donate

Donating items to charity is a great way to ensure they go to a new home to be loved by somebody. Plus you're helping raise money for a good cause. You can donate to thrift stores or pick an local organisations that need contributions (for example, women's shelters often need clothes and home goods). Why not hold a rummage sale and donate the proceeds to your favorite charity?

Giving is incredibly good for your health. It activates the parts of your brain that govern pleasure, social connection and trust – all of which contribute to feeling a 'warm glow'. Scientists have also shown that giving releases endorphins in the brain that fight stress and make us feel positive.

Recycle: reuse and repurpose

You've donated the good stuff and sent the paper and plastic for recycling where possible – but is there anything you can do with the remaining 'waste' before it heads to landfill? It's time to start thinking outside the box (or get online if you're not feeling creative and also fancy seeing some of the wackier ideas) and see a new purpose in things. You'll be surprised what you can breathe new life into:

An old ladder turned on its side and fixed to a wall makes a great rustic/shabby chic bookshelf.

•

Flip an old bookshelf on its back, repaint with bright colors and reuse in the garden as a sand tray for the kids.

•

If you have a wooden cable spool left over after building works, sand it, give it a coat of paint and you've got yourself a new side table or stool.

An old colander can become a hanging basket or, turned upside down, a pendant light.

•

Use old cutlery as plant markers in your garden. Paint labels on to them.

These are just a few ideas, so get your thinking cap on and challenge yourself to create something unique. Make treasure from your trash.

Upcycle

When you upcycle, you reuse something in a way that improves it and gives it more value. Think of this as your chance to get creative. Best of all, creativity creates calmness (and vice versa). Perfect. The two most obvious things to upcycle are clothes and furniture. Whether you plan to keep or to sell items, the process of putting your own creative ideas into action is exciting and therapeutic.

Customize your clothes

Create new outfits from old. You'll be saving money on new clothes and recycling all in one go. The internet is your friend and is packed full of tutorials, but here are a few ideas to get you started (and that don't require a diploma in sewing).

Add sequins, studs or buttons to give any piece of clothing a refresh.

•

Sew patches over areas of clothing that have holes or are getting threadbare. You can get your hands on any patch imaginable, whether you love vintage floral or are a rock star at heart.

•

Update shorts with embellishments – for example, sew a contrasting fabric around the legs and in the pockets.

•

Cut the arms off an old sweater, hem them and – hey presto! – cozy legwarmers.

•

Turn a dress that doesn't fit any more into a kimono. Simply cut down the front center line and hem the cut edges.

•

Embroider a motif to add a striking embellishment to a plain t-shirt.

Revamp your furniture

Do you have a piece of furniture that you don't like or just looks old-fashioned? Don't throw it away. A simple refresh and revamp might be all it needs for you to fall in love with it again. Work within your skill levels, or be bold and learn some new skills. Try these top tips.

Introduce some shabby chic to old drawers, dressers or cupboards. Sand them down and apply a coat of chalk paint. Go over the paint with sandpaper to create the distressed look and add character.

•

Keep it simple. A lick of paint is sometimes all you need to update a piece of furniture and cover the wear and tear. Chalk paint is particularly good if time is at a premium. It can transform something outdated into a modern and stylish addition to your home.

•

Replace the knobs and handles on drawers and cupboards for a quick but very effective update.

•

Use washi tape to spruce up and add a splash of color to furniture. Update a solid chair back with strips of tape, or use it to customize plain vases.

•

Re-upholster a stool or ottoman with the material from an old pair of curtains.

The important thing is to be imaginative and give your creativity free rein. The boost you'll get from this is tremendous. Yes, you'll make mistakes, but you'll also learn new skills along the way, and may even discover a hobby that you can turn to for calm and relaxation.

hoarding – going to the extreme

Tidying and decluttering is a hard process for most people. However, for some, clutter becomes such a problem and takes over their life so much that the physical and psychological barriers to decluttering are immense. You might not even realize that this has happened. Hoarding is recognized as a mental health problem, by itself or as part of a wider issue. This is never anything to be ashamed of. The more you understand why it's happening to you, the better equipped you'll be to deal with it.

What is hoarding?

Hoarding involves keeping lots of items, regardless of their value. For example, you might hoard old newspapers – there's no real purpose in keeping them, but for some reason you do. The reasons for keeping things are very similar to those everyone gives (see the ten classic excuses on page 27), but if you're a hoarder, you'll feel them far more strongly. You will:

get very strong positive feelings when you acquire more items

feel very upset or anxious at the thought of throwing or giving things away

find it very hard to decide what to keep or what to get rid of

be unable to use parts of your home due to the clutter.

Hoarding becomes a problem when your need to keep things causes you distress or interferes with your day-to-day life and your care of yourself. Storing excessive items can even become a fire hazard, blocking your safe exit should an emergency occur. Even when friends and family point out there is a problem, you might not believe them.

What causes hoarding?

No one really knows the answer to this. It's likely to be several factors that have come together to leave you emotionally vulnerable. These could include struggling with difficult feelings (for example after a divorce), being a perfectionist or prone to worry, childhood issues relating to possessions or lack of care, and trauma and loss. Hoarding is a way of building a protective wall around ourselves.

How to start helping yourself

If you know that your hoarding is a problem, don't try and fix it all by yourself. There is support available – you don't need to do it alone.

Talk to someone – a friend, family, your doctor. It is incredibly scary to reach out for support, and you may feel frightened of being judged. Talking is a huge step towards recovery, and you'll be surprised by how much better you feel just by taking this brave step.

•

Connect with support groups in your area where you can talk with and meet people who are experiencing the same as you. An online group is an option if you don't want face-to-face contact. Professional counselling and 'talking therapies' can also be immensely helpful. The main therapy used to treat hoarding is cognitive behavioral therapy (CBT). It focuses on the ways your thoughts and beliefs affect your behavior and feelings.

•

Make a list of questions to ask yourself when you're thinking about acquiring a new item. This can put the brake on. See page 95 for ideas.

•

This is very important: LOOK AFTER YOURSELF. Your physical health affects your emotional health, so get plenty of sleep, exercise and eat well. Find ways to relax that don't involve possessions and/or that get you out of the house. Try walking in nature, watching your favorite movies or catching up with a friend on a beach. Anything that encourages you to relax will help you cope better with stress and feel calmer.

•

Acknowledging you need help is the biggest step. Addressing your hoarding and the underlying causes will take time, so don't be disheartened if change is slow. Remember that each small step is wonderful progress on the road to recovery.

When you're ready, take some small steps. Tidy one small area for just 10 minutes and have a simple goal, for example that you're going to throw one thing away every day. To-do lists are a great way to list what you have and what you're going to do with it. Make a record of your achievements in a diary, or you could take photos of your hard work to remind yourself how well you're doing.

How to support someone who is hoarding

If you're worried about someone, there are things you can do to support them even if they are unwilling to accept your help or acknowledge the problem:

Let them know you are there and can help them when they are ready.

•

Respect their decisions. Even if you don't understand why they keep particular things, remember that the items they hoard feel important to them.

•

Don't take over. Don't touch or move things without their permission. Be gentle.

•

Help them to seek treatment and support.

•

There's lots of information online if they're not ready to approach a professional.

•

Don't pressure them to let you into their home. They might feel anxious about having visitors.

•

Be patient. Even when someone recognizes they need help, it can take time before they feel able to implement changes.

•

Celebrate small successes with them. Remind them that it's one step at a time.

•

Never force them to tidy up or do it for them. This can do more harm than good.

One way to organize your thoughts is to tidy up, even if it's in places where it makes no sense at all.

URSUS WEHRLI

deep clean your headspace

Your 'headspace' is where your mind is at; it's your state of mind. It's the space in your head that gets crowded with the pressures of life and work, leaving you feeling overwhelmed. When you feel that way, it becomes hard to cope with what everyday life throws at you. Even the simplest task can knock you off kilter. In this frenetic modern world, your mental health is as much a priority as your physical health, so keep your headspace clean and tidy.

Read every page of this book!

Everything you'll read about in this book contributes to clearing your mind of stress and encouraging the calm you need to function effectively. Start by working on the area of your life that is making you feel most unhappy.

It could be the state of your living room, an inability to say 'no' at work or friends who seem determined to sap your life force. Tackling one area successfully will give you the confidence to carry on and tackle the next challenge. You'll find yourself sweeping out even the dustiest corners of your headspace. Just imagine having a clear, calm mind that can handle anything it's faced with.

Discover silence (almost)

How often are you ever in a completely silent place? Probably never. The best you can do is seek out somewhere as quiet as possible. Eliminating the stimulation that bombards you daily is like a breath of cool air flowing through your mind. Nature is brilliant for this – it takes you away from the humdrum of the everyday, and uses its own magical sounds to remind you that you're part of a bigger picture.

Quietness gives you the chance to set aside the chatter in your head and to focus. It provides a stillness that, in turn, creates clarity of mind. Take time each day to find somewhere quiet to disconnect and be alone. It's immensely refreshing. And when your mind gets used to achieving a state of calmness, you'll be able to slip into it whenever you need to.

Sleep

A good night's sleep is so vitally important to our physical and mental well-being. Make it one of your top priorities

– you'll feel the difference immediately. It's said that every hour spent asleep before midnight is worth two hours spent asleep after midnight. Fact or fiction – who knows? What we do know is that if you go to bed while your body still has energy to burn, that energy goes towards healing and rebuilding your mind and your body. Sleep helps us to recover from both mental and physical exertion. If you don't get enough of it, you'll experience poor concentration, irritability and increased anxiety. Here's how to get a good night's sleep:

Make your bedroom a calming, clutter-free space (see page 47). Make it a place only for sleeping in, so move the TV and games consoles out!

•

Try to wind down in the hour before you go to bed. Have a bath, listen to soothing music or try relaxing breathing techniques. The more relaxed and freer of the day's worries you are, the easier it will be to sleep.

•

Avoid stimulants like caffeine or heavy meals close to bedtime. Alcohol may make you feel drowsy but it will reduce the quality of your sleep.

Meditation

Meditation is a set of techniques that encourage and develop concentration, clarity, emotional positivity and a sense of calm. It is practised either by focusing attention on a single object (such as a candle flame) or by paying attention to what's in your environment moment, letting the thoughts float by rather than holding on, so that you will naturally feel calmer, starting to pay more attention.

Meditation can have a positive effect on your health and happiness and is easy to do (as you can just 10 minutes can be beneficial). Practised regularly, it can increase your clarity, reduce your feelings of stress and can lower your blood pressure and improve your sleep. Where else is the great start? Try out different meditation techniques to choose what works best for you. If you look online you'll find a whole array of approaches, including guided meditations where someone talks you through a process.

More ideas to try ...

Breathing exercises

Close the world out ...

Write / keep a journal

Practice yoga

Have a massage

Designate a time to think about your worries
and only think about them then

Leave your phone on silent or alarm off

Focus on gratitude

Spend time in nature

Get creative – paint, draw – don't get hung up
on the end part.